Dragonsfire

B715

by the same author

MAGIC MIRROR
and other poems for children

MIDNIGHT FOREST
and other poems

POPCORN PIE
(Mary Glasgow Publications)

HIGGLEDY-HUMBUG
(Mary Glasgow Publications)

edited by Judith Nicholls
WORDSPELLS

WHAT ON EARTH . . .?
Poems with a Conservation Theme

DRAGONSFIRE

and other poems

Judith Nicholls

Illustrated by
Shirley Felts

faber and faber

LONDON · BOSTON

First published in 1990
by Faber and Faber Limited
3 Queen Square London WC1 3AU

Phototypeset by Input Typesetting Ltd, London
Printed in England by
Clays Ltd, St Ives plc

A CIP record for this book is available from the British Library.

ISBN 0–571–14373–3

For Julia and Mike,
Nicky and Adrian,
with love

Contents

In the Beginning . . .

Where salt stones rolled
on starless shores,
where waves roared
under empty skies,
where north winds sighed
to the sleepless moon,
God cried:
Let there be fire!

And *dragon* was born.

Acorn

Acorn,
egg-in-cup;
dizzy drop,
seed-side-up,
on the forest floor.

Winter.
Wet then warm,
sun and storm;
acorn gone,
tree is born:
oak stands there once more!

Journey

I am the acorn
that grew the oak
that gave the plank
the Vikings took
to make a boat
to sail them out
across the seas
to England.

Longship

Chop the oak,
fell the pine!

Row, row
your longship now;
prow to the west
and row, row, row!

Shape the planks,
hammer the nails!
Carve the prow
and set the sails!

Blow, blow,
don't look behind!
Prows to the sunset,
sail with the wind!

Mr Victor

Mr Victor's a travelling man,
    he's cycled Africa, jungle and town,
    he's warmed his feet in a Maori dawn,
    he's eaten snake from his billycan –
        he's a travelling man.

Mr Victor's a storying man,
    he's diced with death in the desert sun,
    cooked crocodile steak in his frying pan;
    he tells a tale like nobody can –
        he's a storying man.

Mr Victor's a long-living man,
    he saw the world when the world began,
    he'll stay around till the end of its span
    (or maybe longer) – at least, that's his plan,
        he's a long-living man.

Riddle

I have seas with no water,
coasts with no sand;
towns but no people,
mountains, no land.

The answer to this riddle is on page 81.

[5]

Timeless

There is no clock in the forest
but a dandelion to blow,
an owl that hunts
when the light has gone,
a mouse that sleeps
till night has come,
lost in the moss below.

There is no clock in the forest,
only the cuckoo's song
and the thin white
of the early dawn,
the pale damp-bright
of a waking June,
the bluebell-light
of a day half-born
when the stars have gone.

There is no clock in the forest.

Song-Thrush

Slug-slayer, snail-snatcher,
soprano turned percussionist,
mad drummer of the rock;
now executioner,
still centre-stage,
beats out her dizzy solo
on execution block.

Caterpillar	*v.*	Snail

Starts fast	One foot
legs ache . . .	starts slow.
Cabbage leaf,	Long way.
quick break!	Food? No!
Eat much,	Keep on,
warm sun . . .	snail's pace.
Snail's passed,	Slowcoach
SNAIL WON!	WINS RACE!

The Purpose
of Keeping a Tortoise

A tortoise
is not a pet I long to keep.
In Summer?
All he does is eat and crawl.
In Winter?
Hide and sleep!

Mosquito

I am
go-as-you-please,
easy houseguest;
I ask no fuss.
My one request,
a little space
to spread my wing.
No lace-edged tablecloth
or grand settee,
no silver dish
or cutlery . . .
Just you
and me.

I am
a simple pet.
I need no lead,
no need for kennel, collar,
cage or vet.
My gentle buzz
is far more sweet
than wasp's or bee's.
I'd never tease or groan,
or eat you out of house and home . . .
A little bite
is quite enough.

So why,
please tell me why
              . . .?

Whalesong

I am
ocean voyager,
sky-leaper,
maker of waves;
I harm no man.

I know
only the slow tune
of turning tide,
the heave and sigh
of full seas meeting land
at dusk and dawn,
the sad whale song.
I harm no man.

Orang-utan

Watch me,
touch me,
catch-me-if-you-can!
I am
soundless,
swung-from-your-sight,
gone with the wind,
shiver of air,
trick-of-the-light.

Watch me,
touch me,
catch-me-if-you-dare!
I hide, I glide,
I stride through air,
shatter the day-star dappled light
over forest floor.
The world's in my grasp!
I am windsong,
sky-flier,
man-of-the-woods,
the arm of the law.

[13]

Wolf

Mine is the howl
that chills the spine
in the forest gloom;
mine is the whine.

Mine is the nose
that breathes in fear
when danger's close;
mine is the ear.

Mine is the fur
the huntsmen trade;
mine is the fur,
I am afraid.

Rhinoceros

There is no rush.
I have slept away
centuries of midday sun,
brushed folded skin
through canes and banyan,
hoof-toed through still grass
with eyes half-closed
to the healing mud
of ancient swamps.
Centuries are mapped on my forehead;
I am not of this time.
My horn beckons . . .

Please, Noah!

Tortoise

I'm slow, Noah,
slow.
Don't put me near
the hare,
the horse's hoof,
the elephant.
Please let me share my room
with someone small:
with mole, light-footed wren
or snail – he cannot stamp
or run. Best of all,
just let me be
alone.

Mouse

Am I the smallest, Noah?
Is it a trap?
Please, I'd like
cheese to gnaw
and nuts to nibble.
I won't quibble
if I have to share
with gerbil, guinea pig
or even rabbit, hare . . .
but please, not *cat*!

Dear Noah,
whatever else,
not *that*!

Sloth

Sleep, Noah,
about my sleep.
I see it's going to be
quite hard for me
to sleep at sea.

You realize, Noah,
for a sloth,
just how important
sleeping is?
Both night
and day!
In fact,
I'd say
. . .

ZZZZZZZ

Counting Sheep

Longhorn
shorthorn
fluffy-tail
ewe
woollyhead
furry-leg
Derby ram too . . .
Woolly sweater
woolly socks
this is how they grew!
Snip it, clip it,
spin it, knit it . . .
just
      for
            YOU!

The Great Gerbil Hunt

I've looked on the table,
I've searched through the fridge;
the cheese box is empty,
I've felt in each vase!
I've checked under carpets,
beneath the settee,
behind every cushion,
below the TV . . .

Yes, I'm *sure* that I closed it,

honestly Dad –
I knew if I didn't
you'd *really* be mad!
Yes, I *know* he was safe
when I last saw him, Mum . . .
Well, I *think* that I'm sure . . .
Yes, I'm *sure* that I am!

That is . . .
I'm sure he'll soon come . . .

LOOK OUT!
DON'T STEP BACK, MUM!

On aurait entendu trotter une souris . . . *

Je suis, moi, je suis
'souris de maison' . . .
T'as raison, mon amie,
t'as raison, t'as raison!

Je cherche et j'adore
les pommes, le Roquefort . . .
Elle cherche le Roquefort;
les pommes elle adore!

J'aime pas le hibou,
je déteste les chats . . .
Et pourquoi pas ça,
détester les chats!

Ici, moi je suis
'souris de maison';
le chèvre et le Brie,
c'est ma vie, c'est ma vie . . .
C'est la vie, mon amie;
c'est sa vie, cette souris!

Les champs? Ça m'ennuie,
je n'en ai pas envie . . .
Pas de champs aujourd'hui;
dans la maison elle vit!

*The translation of this poem is on p. 81.

[21]

. . . mais le chat? Oh, là là!
J'ai grand peur de ça!
Pas une chatte, pas un chat,
elle a grand peur de ça!

Je suis, oui, je suis
'souris de maison' . . .
T'as raison, ma chérie;
t'as raison, t'as raison!

Harvest Hymn

We plough the fields and scatter
our pesticides again;
our seeds are fed and watered
by gentle acid rain.
We spray the corn in winter
till pests and weeds are dead –
who minds a little poison
inside his daily bread?

All good gifts around us
beneath our ozone layer
are safe, oh Lord,
so thank you Lord
that we know how to care.

Something to Do in a Traffic Jam

Dream of
a world where bat
and tiger wander free
and turtles set their courses by
the stars.

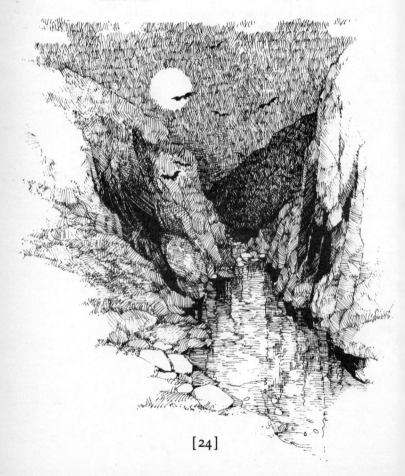

Lord Neptune

Build me a castle,
the young boy cried,
as he tapped his father's knee.
But make it tall
and make it wide,
with a king's throne just for me.

An echo drifted on the wind,
sang deep and wild and free:
Oh you can be king of the castle,
but I am lord of the sea.

Give me your spade,
the father cried;
let's see what we can do!
We'll make it wide
so it holds the tide,
with a fine throne just for you.

He dug deep down
in the firm damp sand,
for the tide was falling fast.
The moat was deep,
the ramparts high,
and the turrets tall and vast.

Now I am king,
the young boy cried,
and this is my golden throne!
I rule the sands,
I rule the seas;
I'm lord of all lands, alone!

The sand-king ruled
from his golden court
and it seemed the wind had died;
but at dusk his throne
sank gently down
in Neptune's rolling tide.

> *And an echo rose upon the wind,*
> *sang deep and wild and free:*
> *Oh you may be king of the castle,*
> *but I am lord of the sea.*

Floating Song

A glimpse of sun
and suddenly –
the world's afloat!

Toddlers gripped in rubber rings,
balding uncles, paleface aunts,
seagulls, poised with folded wings –
all join in the bobbing dance.
Fishing floats and pleasure boats,
pedaloes and reed,
flotsam, jetsam,
cups and pails,
driftwood
(left by winter's gales),
lilos, dinghies,
surfboard sails
and streamers of seaweed.

Rise and fall,
rise and fall,
rise and fall,
drift . . .

Grandpa

blossoms
out and up
over the weary waistband
of his trunks
(they must have seen
a hundred years of wear!)
knots his frayed hankie
like a parachute
to cover fraying hair
then eases down.

In less than half an hour
the *Sunday Mail* has slipped,
its rustle masking
Grandpa's gentle snore.
Sun and the journey,
age and the salt-sea air
return him to an earlier trip
(*When I was young . . .*)
The paper crumples,
slides to the sand
beneath his bulging chair.
Softly he sighs for summers lost;
snores loudly into sleep,
then settles dreams and flesh
more deeply in the canvas,
layer by layer.

Sounds of the Fair

Follow the hurdy-gurdy man!

Pete wanders to the fairground,
drawn by sound:
a barrel organ,
carousel,
a skeleton's unnerving wail
(its echo holds him to the ground) –
the fair is *sound*.

Follow the hurdy-gurdy man!

Pete hesitates
and stares around.
The dodgems? Dipper?
Quickly turns his back
against that lurch of car
on downward track;
now hears what sounds
like distant drums
and follows
half in wonder
half in fear
to join the crowd.
The drums roll on.
They cheer
then gasp out loud
with one accord
as spangled showman
swallows fire and sword.

Follow the hurdy-gurdy man!

Now one last time
Pete turns his back,
heads for a different sound,

the crack of pellets
on the rifle range;
feels for his change
then, fingers trembling,
loads the barrel,
lifts his rifle high.
A bull's-eye first time round?
He'll surely try!

Picnic

George, lend a hand
and spread that cloth,
the sand is everywhere!
Just look at that,
you'd never think
it took hours to prepare!

WAKE UP, GRAMP!
Your food's all out,
get it while you can!
Have a lemonade before
it warms up in the sun.

What is it, Mum?

There's . . .

ham with sand,
and spam with sand,
there's chicken paste
and lamb with sand;
oranges, bananas,
lemonade or tea;
bread with sand
all spread with sand –
at least the sand comes free!
We've crisps with sand
and cake with sand –
it's grand with lunch or tea –
crunch it up,
enjoy it love,
at least we're by the sea!

Fish Pie with Orchestra

You can scrabble with a scallop
        or a lobster,
you can tussle with a mussel
        or a crab;
you can whet your appetite
        with whelks or winkles,
 or dangle from the pier
        for plaice or dab.

You can hear the noisy
        oyster-catcher fishing,
the ringing of the curlew's
        long 'coo-lee';
the tapping of the turnstone
        seeking supper,
the whispered song sung by
        the rolling sea.

Fishmarket

With just one flick the fishman
severs scallops from safe shells,
piles them on slivered ice
to grace the tables roundabout
with mackerel, prawn and plaice.
The staring eyes of speckled trout
outgape his bulging glare;
shuffling through paper-scales
he readjusts one grasping crab
which, from the belly of his stall,
now beckons like some doomed Ahab.

Pass the Pasta!

Spud
is good,
rice
is nice,
but pasta
is faster!

How to Eat a Strawberry

First, sniff –
and then a deep inhale;
note the saliva-flood
round tooth and gum.

Observe seed-studded red,
then feel: Braille promises
through fingertip and thumb
of tastes to come.

Next – bite;
sink deep incisors
into silken flesh –
let juices run!

Close lips;
grasp, roll the prize
through darkened cave
with curling tongue.

Now – *crush*!
Squeeze, savour, pause;
let juice and pulp invade each cell
with taste of summer sun . . .

until the first fruit's gone.

Now take another one!

What's in a Name?

What's in a name?
A rose would look
and smell as sweet
named Nasrat, Rachel, Paramjit.

Give Me Your Name!

Give me your name, and I will . . .

whisper it into the forests,
spell it out in the sands,
I'll shout it over the thunder,
breathe it away on the wind.
I'll spill it over the mountains,
let it echo through the rain;
I'll sing it into a seashell,
if you give me your name.

Name this Child

Joginder, Gurbachan or Amrit,
Ravinder, Rajinder, Swaran,
Satpal, Surinder or Manjit,
Paramjit, Kirpal, Pritam?

Leela, Vaneela or Tara,
Ravi, Rajesh or Rajan,
Sandeep or Gopal or Tushar,
Sushila, Manjula, Poonam?

Gulab, Hussain, Zubaida,
Parveen, Shamim or Hassan,
Jamila, Sharif or Farida,
Nasima, Nasrat, Shazadan?

Van Choc or Van Thai or Thi Kim,
Ken Tsong or Ka Win or Yuk Fan,
Thi My or Van Khai or Thi Thien,
Lai Ling or Lai Ching or Kim Pan?

Jessica, Jocelyn, Lavinia,
Mildred, Matilda or Anne,
Herbert or Humphrey or Hubert,
Letitia, Patricia, Diane?

St David's Day

1st March

In like a lion,
Out like a lamb;
Daffodil, daffy,
Dafydd has come!

Green over white now,
Winter be gone!
Dafydd or Taffy,
St David has come!

May Day

Oak and ivy, sycamore, ash,
Hawthorn, ivy, sycamore, oak.
Wash your face in the May dew,
Wish, then take your chance;
Jack-in-the-Green or Maypole Queen,
Who'll join the Maypole dance?
Hawthorn, sycamore, ivy, oak,
Oak and ivy, sycamore, ash.

What shall we leave by the cottage door?
Drop your branch and say no more!
Pear for the fair, nut for a slut,
Alder for a scowler, hawthorn for a friend;
Bramble for the rambler, plum for the glum –
Drop your branch and run, run, run!
What shall we leave by the cottage door?
Drop your . . . and say no more!

American Independence Day

4th July, 1776

Bonfires, bells and cannon,
gunfire, fife and drum!
Once we owned America –
No more! cried Jefferson.

Raise the flag for liberty,
let the cannon boom!
George III, oh George III,
just look what you have done!

Remembrance Day

11th November

Poppies? Oh, miss,
can I take round the tray?
It's only history next.
We're into '45 –
I *know* who won the war,
no need to stay.

> *Old man wears his flower*
> *with pride, his numbers dying now –*
> *but that's no news.*

Why buy? –
because I'm asked
because a flower looks good
to match my mate
not to seem too mean –
(what's tenpence anyway
to those of us who grew
with oranges, December lettuce
and square fish?)
Yes, I'll wear it –
for a while.
Until it's lost
or maybe picked apart
during some boring television news
and then, some idle moment,
tossed.

Poppies? Who cares
as long as there's
some corner of a foreign field
to bring me pineapple, papaya
and my two weeks' patch of sun? –
But I'll still have one
if you really want.
It isn't quite my scene but then –
at least the colour's fun.

Old man stumbles
through November mud,
still keeps his silence
at the eleventh hour.

Diwali

Ravana's gone,
the demon king has done!
Now once again
with feasting and with prayer
we light a thousand guiding lamps
to welcome Rama here
and bring good fortune
for the coming year.

Seder

Why celebrate with bitter herbs,
salt tears of still-remembered slaves
and (though there's time now
for less hasty ways)
this joyless bread?

The salt reminds us still
of parting seas,
and, though there's time now,
once was none;
whilst plague took
Egypt's eldest sons
we brought to safety
our firstborn.

Pass over, Death;
Pass over, Death;
Passover . . .

Clown

Pocketful of water-pistols,
eggs to bounce or throw or drop;
bucketful of spilling water,
pants that droop and shoes that flop.
Broken ladder, stilts, a bike
without a seat and just one wheel . . .

Does he *really* like being laughed at,
underneath his painted smile?

Christmas Story

Once upon a time, children,
and it was a very long time ago,
there were three men . . .

What were they called, miss?

We don't know, Andrew,
what they were called,
where they came from,
where they went.
We just know that
they were shepherds . . .

What's a shepherd, miss?

A shepherd, Andrew,
is someone who looks after . . .

Please, miss . . .

Someone who looks after . . .

*My Uncle Bill had to look after me,
last night, miss!*

SHEEP, Andrew, sheep!
A shepherd cares for sheep!
Now one night,
on a dark hillside . . .

I don't like it when it's dark, miss!

On this hillside . . .

Do you think they were scared, miss?

I don't think so, Andrew.
These shepherds had been there
on the hillside,
many nights before.
They talked quietly, together,
under the stars . . .

YOU said I could have a star, miss!
For my picture. You PROMISED!

Quietly together,
under the stars,
watching their sheep . . .

Why didn't they watch Batman, miss?
Were they too scared?

This was a *very* long time ago, Andrew.
There was NO Batman.
No Batman, no Muppets,
no Blue Peter, no Grange Hill,
no Blockbusters, no Ghostbusters,
NO television!
They watched their SHEEP . . .

My Dad told me to count sheep
when I didn't want to go to bed.
Sheep'll make you sleep,
he said!

I know just what he means, Andrew!
They watched their sheep . . .

[46]

WHY did they need to watch them, miss?

To keep them safe, Andrew,
just like your Mum and Dad keep you safe.
To stop them getting lost . . .

My Mum once lost me, miss!

She must have been very . . . worried, Andrew!
But she found you again, just like . . .

*It was in Woolworths, miss,
at Christmas . . .*

Just like a shepherd . . .

*I was scared, miss,
I was REALLY scared!*

Just . . .

*I didn't know where she was!
But I didn't cry, miss,
really I didn't . . .*

JUST like a shepherd,
rescuing his sheep with his crook . . .

*My Uncle Bill's a crook, miss!
Dad says! Dad says he once . . .*

THANK you, Andrew!
Perhaps we should all sing the song we know,
about these shepherds watching their sheep
on the quiet hillside.

Then, maybe,
we could choose some children
to be the shepherds
in our Christmas play . . .

Oh, PLEASE miss,
let ME be a shepherd.
If you want a crook
I could bring my Un . . .

THANK YOU, ANDREW!

Tongue in Cheek

My heart's in my mouth,
my brain has been washed –
my tongue's in my cheek.

I've a chip on my shoulder,
I've brought up a child –
I'm feeling quite weak.

I've paid through the nose,
made a pig of myself –
you should take a peek.

I'm pulling a face,
here's a piece of my mind –
I really can't speak.

My eyes are the size
of three stomachs or more –
my tongue's in my cheek.

Bodywork

Fibula, tibia, tarsals and rib,
clavical, cranium, spine;
whatever the outside appearance,
all praise to the inner design!

I've a mandible, patella, metatarsal,
I have biceps, I have triceps and a brain;
a pulmonary artery takes blood one way,
then back it comes through pulmonary vein.
There's retina and anvil, epiglottis,
oesophagus and pancreas and tongue;
how could I cope without my parathyroids,
Eustachian tube or diaphragm or lung?

Fibula, tibia, tarsals and rib,
clavical, cranium, spine;
whatever I seem from the outside,
you can't fault the inner design!

Hair-Raiser

Why are there hairs in your nose, Daddy;
why all those hairs in your nose?
Those are vibrissae, my darling;
vibrissae, as everyone knows!

Why are there hairs on your chest, Daddy;
why are there no hairs on mine?
Hairs on your chest will come later, my son;
hairs on the chest take some time!

Why's there no hair on your head, Daddy;
why not a hair on your head?
Hair on the head is an optional extra –
now eat up your dinner, then *bed*!

And How Are You . . .?

How am I?
I'm not so bad,
the ankle's just about all right
(except at night)
but shoulder . . .
that's a different tale.
You hadn't heard?
It was a nasty fall!
I went with quite a whack,
quite set me back –
I've never *known*
such throbbing!
Lucky not to smash the bone.
But still . . .
       I mustn't moan.

Of course,
this sinusitis doesn't help!
They did my nose last year, you know.
I'll never breathe the same!
Then tonsillitis
and a nasty bout of 'flu . . .
What can you do,
I ask myself,
when you're alone?
The family's gone,
all moved from home.
I wish . . . but no,
       I mustn't groan.

[53]

You're going away?
I'd like to go, of course,
but with *my* legs . . .
I never stray too far.
You see that nasty scar
where they tied up the vein?
You'd never *dream*
there'd be such pain
from such a simple job.
But otherwise . . .
          I can't complain.

Till Death . . .

The world
is full of it,
there is no fee. Comes free
but with no long-term guarantee,
that's life!

Evolution

I met my foe the other day;
we fought with fist and knee.
We grappled, shouldered,
kicked and roared
till finally, our limbs subdued,
each slunk away.

I met my foe the other day;
he came with fist
and I with sword.
I answered flesh
with sharpened steel,
he sank without a word.

I met my foe the other day;
I brought my dainty gun.
He bared his sword to greet me;
one finger crooked,
my foe was gone.

I saw my foe the other day –
no more than just a blur
across a smoky battlefield.
I saw him fall . . .

                or was it *her*?

I didn't even see my foe –
no faces, no distress.
I pressed the button quickly
and found a wilderness.

Jairus' Daughter

Rush presses at my back,
distracts from smell of bread,
hot women, dust.
Wailing drifts over
with dovecall, donkey's bray
and rustling fig.
Through closed eyes I know
my father's stoop,
my mother's woe.

Sun splinters
the narrow lattice,
fills the room;
slowly reaches
hand and hair and eyes.
Hush falls like a mist
on all the women round.
Morning has come;
I reach,
I rise.

Juggler

With arms unhinged
and blurred in speed,
knees flexed, he casts
to front and back.
Eyes pivot; all is lost
except for red on black
as circling torches
burn a track of curving air
through darkened skies;
leave us to wonder who
is earthbound still, who flies –
the tosser or the tossed.

Icarus

Down through curling heat
from a still sea
the wax wings beat in dizzy fall,
melt into skewbald light then
trail white stars in a noon sky.

The Cyclops' Revenge

Hear me, Poseidon,
hail-thrower, wave-maker,
brewer of foam and flood,
great god of the sea!
Send me winds, send me rain,
send me hurricane, storm;
send me tempests too black
for the skies to contain!
May Charybdis' wild waters
hiss with your fury,
close round Odysseus
and his fine men;
may they lurch from their ships
may they sink to your sands;
may they never set foot
on their own lands
again!

The Dare

1
Steep banks
and oozing mud
are all I see below;
no friends, just voices jeering: 'Yes –
or no?'

2
Go on,
I dare you, jump!
Mud lapped with water swims
before my eyes; behind, in dreams,
I drown.

Skateboard

Car park,
Sunday.

Ollying,
skip-and-hop;
downhill,
can't stop!
World spins,
board high;
hit kerb,
sparks fly!
Wheels turn,
knees scrape;
world spins,
can't wait . . .

Sunday,
car park,

SKATEBOARD!

How to Make a Patchwork Cushion

Silk and satin linen rags
Satin linen rags and silk
Linen satin silk and rags
Rags and satin linen silk
Silk and linen satin rags
Linen rags and satin silk
Satin linen silk and rags

Stitch it up in patchwork bags!

Riddle

I have notes but no paper,
flats but no home;
hammers, no tool box,
no words but a song.

The answer to this riddle is on p. 81.

Magic

A web
captures the storm:
glass beads, safe in fine net,
gather sunlight as they sway in
high winds.

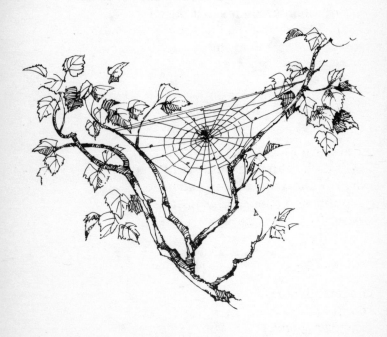

Magician

whose top hat cages seven doves
in whose sleeve burrows mouse or rat
who severs young girl, neck from head
and shuffles with a pack of hearts
who finds and takes where there was none
whose wandering glove on wandering hand
can lose in seconds what once was –
who dares have dealings with this man?

School Visit

The Great Merlanda's here today
with tricks and traps and spells;
there's not a murmur in the hall,
you'd hear a speck of stardust fall
except

    for Jim

        who

fidgets, fiddles,
whispers, wriggles,
sniggers, giggles,
won't sit still

    till

        at last

[63]

The Great Merlanda,
footsteps ringing,
cloak a-swinging,
strides right down
past seated pupils
reaches Jim's row,
simply yells . . .

IF YOU DON'T SIT IN YOUR CHAIR, BOY,

I'll . . .

turn you into a rabbit
and stuff you in my hat,
I'll lock you up in my bottomless box
or places worse than that!
I'll turn you into the six of spades
and deal you out to the Head;
I'll saw you in two then tie up the bits
in a granny-knot, I said!
I'll turn you into a handkerchief
or a mouse to play with my cat!
If you can't sit still
    RIGHT NOW
            on that chair . . .

Said Jim,
            'I'll do just that!'

What Goes On in the Cloakroom

Stevie is feeling the pockets,
Simon's come for his gum;
Jenny's supposed to be on research
but she's really on the run
from Jilly, who's on the way out next
pretending to hold her knee
which is dripping with red
(from the paintpot)
and she smears it over me.
Timmy has asked to leave the room
but catches his hair on a peg –
or was it Jilly who wound it round
as he tripped against her leg?
Stevie has found an egg sandwich
and a packet of crisps and much more.
He settles down for a quiet munch
when who should come through the door
to disturb his nuts and cheese and ham
but . . .

Sir!

SCRAM!

Poem, Please!

What, *now*?
Big strain;
no thoughts,
brain drain!
Spine shivers,
fingers twist;
think fast,
make list?
Writer's block,
head aches;
pencil lost,
arm shakes!
Teacher's voice:
'Finished yet?'
Heart sinks,
hands sweat!
Quick, now,
let's go . . .
'Time's up!'
Oh,
      NO!

The Bookshop

Welcome to the bookshop,
the books are yours to buy!
We've big ones, small ones, funny, sad
tales to make you cry . . .

but
        DON'T TOUCH THE BOOKS!

We've poems, stories, sagas
to make you catch your breath . . .
tales of love and tales of war,
tales of life and death . . .

just
        DON'T TOUCH THE BOOKS!

Toys and television
are both things of the past –
reading is the thing today,
reading pleasures last . . .

but
    please
        DON'T TOUCH THE BOOKS!

Hermitage Woods

Who was the hermit of Hermitage Woods,
and why did he walk alone?
Was his bed of moss and his roof a star,
was his pillow stone?

Was the hoot of the owl his lullaby,
the wind in the oak his song?
Was the moon his only candle,
when day was done?

Who was the hermit of Hermitage Woods,
and why was he there?
When he smiled, who shared his laughter;
when he cried, who could hear?

Was the scent of pine in his winter breath?
Did his eyes burn with the sun?
What taste of mists swirled in his throat
and round his tongue?

Who *was* the hermit of Hermitage Woods,
who walked at dusk and dawn?
Where are the oaks which sheltered him?
Where has he gone?

4 p.m.

Paint dry,
pens gone;
chalk dust
drifts down.

Pawns still,
knights wait;
kings sleep,
checkmate!

Books closed,
maths done;
ghosts stir
alone.

Camping Out

Can we sleep out in the tent, Dad?
Go on, just him and me!
It's a full moon,
not a cloud in sight!
We'll be quiet as
mice when the cat's about –
oh, *please* let us stay the night?

You can pitch your tent down the garden
by the lilac, or just behind;
but mind you're in by midnight
if you're going to change your mind.
The key will be out till twelve,
but not a second more.
I don't want prowlers after that –
at twelve I lock the door!

Great, Dad!
We'll be out till morning –
you've never let us before!
We'll fetch all we need
before it's dark
then you can lock your door.

The key will be out till twelve,
I said, but not a second more!

Now, what do we need?
Water, jug,
toothpaste, mug,
towel, rug,
toothbrush . . .

*Since when were you so keen
on keeping clean?*

You can't camp out down the Amazon
without the proper gear.
We could be here a *year*,
exploring dark Brazil
until – who knows?

*All right, a torch then,
I suppose. Sleeping bags.
Pillows?*

There's no room.
Mosquito nets come first,
and books to read
by torch or moon.
Pencils, notebooks.
Sweaters – two at least.
And don't forget the midnight feast!

*What do explorers eat?
Will crisps and apples do,
with peanut-butter sandwiches,
bananas, orange juice,
and baked beans for the stew?*

They'll do!

*

I wish we'd brought a pillow.
It's really dark.
I thought you said no cloud?
Should we close the flap –
to keep mosquitoes out, I mean?

Or leopards!

. . . and to keep us warm.
There goes that flash again.
The air feels heavy.
P'rhaps a jungle storm?
Listen!
Can you hear – a breeze?
Something's rustling,
quickly, *freeze!*

*Could it be
some deadly snake,
uncoiling for . . .*

For goodness sake,
it's only trees!

*Oh, look!
What IS that shadow up above?
I'm sure I saw it move!*

It's nothing,
just the lilac.
Or some bat or owl
out on the prowl
for supper too.

TOOWHIT, TOOWHOO!

No need to jump,
it's nearer me than you!

I didn't jump!
What time is it,
only five to midnight?
Just wondered.
Thought it might be more.

I DON'T WANT PROWLERS AFTER THAT,
AT TWELVE I LOCK THE DOOR . . . !

Aren't you cold?
I wish we'd brought more blankets,
the jungle's not so hot
when sun's gone down;
we didn't think of that.

Not cold, just hungry.
It's great out here,
but as for food –
we should have brought much more.
Explorers need their sustenance.
Another time, we'll plan it better . . .

But meantime,

RACE YOU TO THE DOOR!

Fearless

Ghosts and foul ghoulies
I can withstand;
skeletons, witches,
I'd take by the hand.
A poltergeist's welcome,
a dragon is grand
BUT . . .
    Who'll move the spider?

Dinosaurs, krakens –
such friendly ways!
Octopus, jellyfish,
Martians from space.
The centaur, a phoenix
I'd look in the face
BUT . . .
    Who'll move the spider?

Dusk

The beach has cleared.
All but a stalwart few
(young sweethearts,
tramps or local dogs)
have emptied shoes
of stones and sand,
retreated to the prom.
With hands and spirit warmed
by local fish and chips,
each one reviews his day.

The sun is low across the bay,
changes the shape of things,
casts magic over what was not.
The beach-day's litter
fades into a kindly gloom;
the clock-tower, dull at noon,
now turns to magic Camelot
and visions of enchanted nights
are stirred as, one by one,
a thousand wandering stars
give way to endless lights.

Earthset

Night spreads like purple heather
over wasteland sky
and marbled earth rolls gently into sleep.

Windsong

I am the seed
that grew the tree
that gave the wood
to make the page
to fill the book
with poetry.

Two Answers and a Translation

Riddle, page 5: A map.

On aurait entendu trotter une souris . . . (You could have heard a mouse scurrying . . .), page 21:

The rhymes, repetitions and other devices that make this a poem in French are difficult to capture in English, but here is a rough translation:

I am a 'house-mouse' . . . *You're right, my friend, you're right!* I look for and I love apples and Roquefort cheese . . . *She looks for Roquefort; she loves apples!* I don't like the owl, I hate cats . . . *And what's wrong with that, hating cats?* Here I am a 'house-mouse'; goat's-milk cheese and Brie, they're my life . . . *That's life, my friend; that's the life for this mouse!* Fields? they bore me, I don't hanker for them . . . *No fields today; this mouse lives in the house!* But the cat? Oh dear! I'm really afraid of that! *No cats or tomcats, please, she really is afraid of them!* I am, yes, a 'house-mouse' . . . *You're right, my darling, you're right!*

Riddle, page 61: A piano.